LIFE'S LITTLE APPLE COOKBOOK:

101 Apple Recipes

by Joan Bestwick

THE ADVOCATE COLLECTION

Life's Little Apple Cookbook
101 Apple Recipes
by Joan Bestwick

Copyright 2003
by Avery Color Studios, Inc.
ISBN# 1-892384-22-1
Library of Congress Control Number: 2003108104
First Edition 2003

Published by
Avery Color Studios, Inc.
Gwinn, Michigan 49841

Cover photo by Michael Prokopowicz
Michael's Photographics, Gwinn, Michigan

Proudly printed in U.S.A.

Table of Contents

This book is dedicated to my Lord and Savior Jesus Christ. My buddies Judy Adrian, Holly Scott, Pat Hanna, Cheryl Goul and Sheri Grzeskowiak. My sisters-in-law Peggy Manning, Sherry Morrison, Kim Hammond, Jeraldean Worachek and Tina Werkmann, and to the Tuesday Inter Faith Bible Study Group, you'll never meet more awesome, loving, Godly women in the world.

ello,

I feel very blessed. My life has been so rich and full, even though there were some mountains and pitfalls in my path.

Growing up in the country is what I will cherish. Spring time with the smell of apple blossoms permeating the air. The sounds of honey bees gathering nectar from the fruit blossoms to carry back to the bee hives so we can later enjoy the sweet honey, yum, yum.

When I was growing up, my grandparent's trees held apples we called sheepsnose, transparents, delicious and Dutch apple. The Dutch apple made the most awesome, sweet, pink applesauce in the world.

Where we live now, our backyard is also full of fruit trees. The old apple orchard, and I mean an old orchard, produces delicious transparent and sheepsnose. There are apple trees that we have no idea what they are, the original owner loved to graft trees, so who knows what has been grafted on many of these trees, but they are good apples.

Apples are versatile, healthy and delicious. What would fall be like without apple harvests, carmel apples, cider, pies, hayrides, scarecrows and bonfires? Parties where you're bobbing for apples in a water filled wash tub or with a partner trying to eat the apple swinging on a string.

Food is a way for family and friends to come together for fellowship and communication. Remember an apple a day keeps the doctor away, so buy lots of books and pass them out to family and friends. God Bless you.

Joan

Apple Varieties
There are so many varieties of apples now. A general rule is that tart apples are best for cooking or baking, such as:
Rome Beauty, Imperial Granny Smith, Golden Delicious and Northern Spy.
Apples like Jonathan, Empires, Ida Red, McIntosh, Red Delicious and Cortland are good for eating or salads.

Baking Tips
When using a glass pie dish, place it on a metal baking tray to help cook and brown the crust thoroughly.

Apples
1 pound of apples equals: 4 small apples, 3 medium apples or 2 large apples

1 pound apples equals: 2 3/4 cups sliced or 3 cups diced

2 medium apples = 1 cup grated

Pared: means to peel the apple

Core: to remove the core (the center containing the seeds) of the apple

Apple Facts
An average apple contains 80-90 calories.

Apples are high in fiber and pectin. They contain almost no fat or saturated fat and are sodium free.

They are a good source of vitamins A, B & C and contain minerals like iron and potassium. It is also said a diet containing lots of apples, helps to reduce blood cholesterol levels.

Apples also act like a natural toothbrush. They clean your breath, brush your teeth and massage your gums.

How to buy and store apples

Look for bright colored apples, no matter what color they are, (red, green or yellow). If they have a bright green undercast, they are not ripe enough. If the apples are dull, with a yellowish green tinge, they are overripe.

Feel the apple for firmness and check the skin for a firm feeling. Avoid apples that have bruises, blemishes and breaks.

Store apples in a cool, dry place or in the refrigerator crisper. Apples ripen faster at room temperature. When storing apples, keep them away from strong smelling foods, because they will pick up those flavors. Do not freeze apples. Apples will store for about 1 month.

BEVERAGES, DIPS
AND APPETIZERS

The greatest calamity is not to have failed;
but to have failed to try.

Hot Buttered Cider

1 gallon apple cider
1 cup brown sugar
1/2 cup butter
1 stick cinnamon
2 teaspoon whole cloves

In a heavy pot, bring the apple cider to a boil. Add the remaining ingredients and simmer over low heat, stirring until sugar dissolves. Strain and serve.

Apple-Limeade Juice

1 6-ounce can thawed limeade concentrate
1 32-ounce bottle apple juice
1 cup cold water
crushed ice
maraschino cherries

In a large pitcher, combine the limeade, apple juice and water. Mix well. Pour over crushed ice into serving glasses and top with maraschino cherries.

Apple Sunny Punch

1-1/2 quarts cranberry juice
1 quart apple juice
1/4 cup orange juice
2 6-ounce cans frozen lemonade
4-1/4 cups water
crushed ice
grapefruit sections
lemon slices

Make sure all your juices are chilled well. Pour all the liquids into your punch bowl and mix. Put the ice in and garnish with the grapefruit and lemon. Serves 20.

Hot Cider Treat

2 quarts apple cider
2 teaspoons allspice
2 teaspoons whole cloves
4 sticks cinnamon
12 thin lemon slices (optional)

In a large pot over medium-low heat, combine all of the ingredients except the lemon slices. Cover and simmer slowly for 20 minutes. Remove from heat and strain. Keep warm. Serve hot and with the lemon slices if desired. Serves 6.

Quick Cran-Apple Punch

2 quarts chilled apple cider
2 cups cranberry juice
2 teaspoons lemon juice
4 cups ginger ale, chilled
crushed ice

In a large pitcher or punch bowl, combine the apple cider, cranberry juice and lemon juice. Mix well and chill. Just before serving, stir again and add the ginger ale and crushed ice. Serve in punch glasses.

Apple Cider Dip

4 cups apple cider
1 teaspoon vanilla
1-1/2 cups sugar
1 tablespoon lemon juice
2 tablespoons unsalted butter
2 tablespoons heavy cream

In a medium saucepan over medium-high heat, add the apple cider and vanilla. Cook stirring frequently. Reduce this liquid to about 1 cup. It takes about 30 minutes. To this reduced mixture add the sugar and lemon juice. Cook until this mixture turns a deep amber color, approximately another 10 minutes. Remove the mixture from the heat and strain. To this add the butter and stir in the cream. Serve at room temperature. Makes about 2 cups.

Apple Dip

1 8-ounce package of cream cheese, softened
3/4 cup packed brown sugar
1 tablespoon vanilla extract
1/2 cup chopped peanuts
6 apples, cut into wedges

In a small bowl, beat the cream cheese, brown sugar and vanilla until smooth. Spread this mixture on a small serving plate and top with the nuts. Serve the dip with the apple wedges.

Apple Shrimp Cocktail

3/4 pound cooked large shrimp
2 cups diced red apple
1 tablespoon lemon juice
6 lettuce leaves
2 cups shredded lettuce
1/2 cup chopped celery
1 teaspoon salt
1/3 cup mayonnaise
6 cocktail glasses

Take your shrimp and cut them lengthwise and set aside. In a small bowl toss the apples and lemon juice. Place a lettuce leaf in each cocktail glass. Place 1/3 cup shredded lettuce in each cocktail glass. Then alternate the shrimp and apple in each glass dividing into equal amounts around the inside edge of each glass. In a small bowl combine the celery, salt, mayonnaise and mix well. Drop by equal amounts in each glass, serve.

BUTTERS, SAUCES
AND WHAT NOT

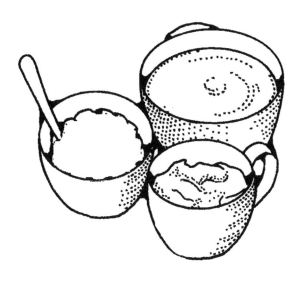

*It's just as easy to look for the good things
in life rather than the bad.*

Apple Butter–The Old Way

5 pounds of tart apples, peeled, cored and cut up
3 cups apple cider
4 cups sugar
3 teaspoons cinnamon
1 teaspoon cloves

In a heavy pot, add your apples and cider. Bring this to a boil and then reduce the heat and simmer. Cover for about 25 minutes stirring occasionally.

Remove the apples and puree. Add the sugar and spices. Mix well.

Pour the apple puree mixture into a shallow baking dish and bake at 300° for 2 hours or until thick enough to hold its shape when stirred. Pour into hot sterile jars and seal.

Crockpot Apple Butter

1 large crockpot filled with pared, cored and chopped apples
4 cups sugar
4 to 6 teaspoons cinnamon
1 teaspoon cloves (optional)
1 teaspoon salt

Mix all of the ingredients except the apples in a bowl. Pour the sugar mixture over the apples in the crockpot. Cover and cook all day stirring occasionally mashing down as you stir. Cook until dark and thick. Pour into hot, sterile jars and seal.

Sweet Potato Butter

6 cups sweet potatoes, peeled and diced
2 cups tart apples, peeled and diced
4 cups water
2/3 cup orange juice concentrate
1/2 cup packed dark brown sugar
1-1/2 teaspoons ground cinnamon
1 teaspoon ground nutmeg
1/4 to 1/2 teaspoon ground cloves

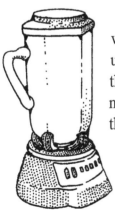

In a saucepan, combine all of the ingredients and mix well. Bring this mixture to a boil. Reduce heat and simmer uncovered for 2 to 2-1/4 hours or until the mixture is thickened and about one cup of liquid remains. Stir this mixture occasionally while cooking. In a blender, process the mixture and place into containers. Chill for at least 2 hours before serving. You can store this mixture for up to 2 weeks. I do not recommend freezing because it breaks down and becomes watery. Makes 4 cups.

The Basic Recipe For Apple Sauce

To me applesauce is a preference. Some people like it smooth, some chunky. Then it comes to the taste as to how tart or sweet they like it.

5 pounds of cooking apples
3 cups of water
1 to 1-1/2 cups of sugar

Peel, pare, core and chop up the apples. Put then in a kettle with the water. Cook over medium heat stirring frequently to prevent sticking. Cook the apples down until they are soft.

Now some people like smooth applesauce. If so, put the apples threw a sieve or processor. For chunky or not so smooth, all I do is as the apples start getting soft in the kettle, I use a potato masher and start mashing them. After mashed or sieved, start adding your sugar to taste. You can either serve warm or cold. You can also put the hot apple sauce in hot, sterilized jars and seal using a hot water bath.

Honey Apple Sauce

6 medium apples, pared and sliced
1 cup water
1/3 cup honey
dash of cinnamon

Over medium heat, in a medium saucepan, add your apples and water. Cook for about 15 minutes or until the apples are tender. Put the apple mixture through a sieve. Stir in the honey and garnish with cinnamon. Serves 6.

Spiced Apple Slices

2-2/3 cups sugar
2 cups white vinegar
2/3 cup water
2 teaspoons whole cloves
1 6-inch cinnamon stick
1/2 teaspoon salt
6 drops red food coloring
6 large apples

In a pot over medium heat, combine the sugar, vinegar, water, cloves, cinnamon, salt and food coloring. Bring to a boil. Pare, core and quarter the apples. Slice each quarter into thirds lengthwise. Add the apples to the hot syrup and cook until the apples are transparent. Pack the apples in hot sterilized jars and cover with the boiling syrup. Seal the jars in a hot water bath. This recipe only makes 2 pints, so you may want to increase the recipe for more jars.

Canned Apple Pie Filling

4-1/2 cups sugar
1 cup cornstarch
2 teaspoons ground cinnamon
1/4 teaspoon ground nutmeg
1 teaspoon salt
10 cups water
3 tablespoons lemon juice
2-3 drops red food coloring
5-1/2 to 6 pounds tart apples, peeled, cored and sliced

In a large pot, blend the first five ingredients. Stir in the water and cook over medium heat, stirring occasionally, until thick and bubbly. Add lemon juice and food coloring. Pack the apples into the canning jars, leaving 1 inch head space. Then add to this the hot syrup leaving 1/2 inch head space. Make sure the syrup is distributed into the fruit. Wipe the tops of the jars with a cloth to remove the filling. Top the jars with the canning lids and rings. Process in a boiling hot water bath, pints 15 minutes, quarts 20 minutes. This makes 6 quarts. Try to use wide mouth canning jars for easier removal of the fruit.

Apple Almond Relish

4 medium tart apples, peeled and chopped
2 cups sugar
1 cup chopped dried apricots
1 cup golden raisins
1/4 cup white vinegar
2 tablespoons grated orange peel
1/2 cup slivered almonds, toasted

In a large saucepan, combine all the ingredients except the almonds. Bring this mixture to a boil, stirring constantly. Reduce the heat and simmer for 20-30 minutes, stirring frequently until thickened. At the end of cooking time, add the almonds. Makes 4 cups of relish.

Apple Conserve

3 pounds ripe apples
5-1/2 cups sugar
1/3 cup cider vinegar
1/2 cup currants
1/2 cup walnuts
1/2 cup red cinnamon candy
2 tablespoons lemon juice
1/2 bottle pectin

Wash, pare and core the apples. Chop coarsely. Measure 4 cups chopped apples into kettle. Add the remaining ingredients except pectin. Heat to a boil, stirring constantly. Boil for 1 minute. Remove from the heat immediately and stir in the pectin. Mix for 5 minutes and skim off the excess foam. Pour into clean, hot jars leaving 1/4 inch head space. Put on the canning lids and process for 10 minutes in a hot water bath. Yield: 10 half-pints.

Cinnamon Apple Jelly

7 cups unsweetened bottled apple juice
1 package (1-3/4 ounce) powdered fruit pectin
2 teaspoons butter (no substitutes)
1 cup red-hot candies
9 cups sugar

In a large kettle over high heat, add the apple juice, fruit pectin and butter. Bring this mixture to a boil stirring constantly. Stir in the candies until dissolved. Stir in the sugar and return to a full boil. Boil for 1 minute stirring constantly. Remove from the heat and skim off the foam. Pour the hot mixture into hot sterilized jars leaving 1/4 inch head space. Wipe the tops of the jars clean and place the lids and rings on the jars. Process for 5 minutes in a boiling hot water bath. Makes 13 half-pints.

SALADS

*People seldom want to
walk over you until you lie down.*

Apple Coleslaw

4 cups (about 1/2 a head) red cabbage, shredded
1/2 cup onion, chopped
2 Granny Smith apples, cut into match sticks
1/3 cup sour cream
1/3 cup mayonnaise
3 tablespoons apple cider vinegar
1/2 teaspoon salt
1/2 teaspoon sugar
1/2 teaspoon caraway seeds (optional)
1/4 teaspoon pepper

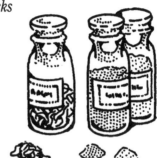

In a large bowl, combine the cabbage, onion and apples, set aside. In a small bowl whisk together the remaining ingredients until smooth. Pour this mixture over the cabbage mixture and toss to mix well and chill. This slaw will hold up for two days refrigerated.

Sweet Pickle Chicken Salad

1 cup cooked chicken, chopped
1 apple, peeled, cored and diced
1/2 cup sweet pickles, chopped
1/4 cup mayonnaise
salt, pepper and paprika, to taste
lettuce Leaves

Mix first 5 ingredients together in a bowl. Serve over the lettuce leaves.

Apple Nut Jello Salad

1 3-ounce package lime flavored gelatin
1-1/4 cups boiling water
3/4 cup cold water
1 tablespoon lemon-lime juice
1/8 teaspoon salt
1/2 cup celery, finely chopped
1-1/2 cups apple, chopped
1/2 cup pecans, chopped
1/4 cup walnuts, chopped
lettuce leaves

Dissolve gelatin in boiling water. Add cold water, lemon-lime juice and salt. Chill until thick but not set. Add celery, apples, pecans and walnuts. Mix well. Pour into a 1-quart mold and chill until set. Unmold on lettuce leaves. Serves 6.

Apple Carrot Salad

1 cup carrots, shredded
3 cups apples, diced
1/3 cup raisins
1/3 cup walnuts, chopped
2/3 cup mayonnaise
1 tablespoon lemon juice
1/8 teaspoon salt

In a bowl, combine all the ingredients. Toss to mix well. Serves 6.

Waldorf Salad

2 cups apples, diced
1/2 teaspoon lemon juice
1 cup seedless green grapes
1 cup celery, diced
1/2 cup walnuts, chopped
1/2 cup mayonnaise
1/2 cup whipped cream

In a medium bowl, toss the lemon juice and the apples. Add the grapes, celery and walnuts. Combine this well. Stir in the mayonnaise and whipped cream and chill. Serves 6.

Cinnamon Apple Salad

6 apples
1/2 cup red cinnamon candies
1/4 cup sugar
2 cups water
2 tablespoons walnuts, chopped
10 dates, pitted and chopped
1/2 cup pineapple, diced
1/4 cup salad dressing

Pare and core the apples and leave whole. In a saucepan add the candies, sugar and water. Cook until the sugar is dissolved. Add the whole apples until they are transparent but not soft, remove and chill. Combine the walnuts, dates, pineapple and salad dressing and stuff the center of the apples with this mixture. Serve on lettuce.

Tuna Apple Salad

2 cans (6-1/2 to 7 ounces each) tuna
2 cups apples, diced
1/2 cup celery, chopped
1/2 cup mayonnaise or salad dressing
1/4 cup raisins (optional)
1 tablespoon lemon juice
lettuce

Drain tuna. In a bowl, add all the ingredients except the lettuce. Combine them well and serve on a bed of lettuce. Serves 6. Instead of raisins you can use dried cherries or cranberries for a tart kick.

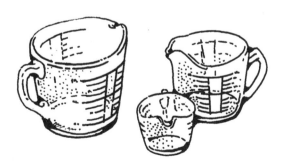

Apple Cherry Salad

3/4 cup banana, sliced
1 cup apples, diced
1 tablespoon lemon juice or orange juice
3/4 cup dark sweet cherries, pitted and halved
3/4 cup drained Mandarin orange sections
2/3 cup light corn syrup (optional)

In a small bowl, combine the banana slices and apples with the juice and coat well. Then in a medium bowl combine all of the fruits and gently toss. Cover and chill. If you choose, just before serving, top the fruit with the corn syrup. Serves 6.

Coleslaw

3-1/2 cups cabbage, finely shredded
1 cup apples, diced
1 cup cucumbers, diced
1/4 cup raisins
2/3 cup mayonnaise
1 tablespoon lemon juice
1/2 tablespoon vinegar
1/2 teaspoon salt
1/8 teaspoon sugar

In a medium bowl, combine cabbage, apples, cucumber and raisins. Toss to mix. In a small bowl blend mayonnaise, lemon juice, vinegar, salt and sugar. Pour mayonnaise dressing over the mixture. Toss to coat well and chill. Serves 6.

Peanut Butter Apple Salad

2 cups tart apples, cubed
2 cups seedless grapes, halved
2 cups Bartlett pear, cubed
1 cup miniature marshmallows
1/3 cup cold evaporated milk
1/2 teaspoon sugar
1/2 teaspoon vanilla extract
3 tablespoons mayonnaise
3 tablespoons creamy peanut butter
1/2 cup or more mixed nuts, chopped

In a large bowl, combine the fruits and marshmallows. In a chilled mixing bowl, beat the evaporated milk until frothy. Then add the sugar and vanilla. Beat in the mayonnaise and peanut butter. Pour this over the fruit mixture and gently stir until well coated. Cover and refrigerate. Just before serving, add the nuts if desired. Serves 10 to 15 people depending on serving sizes.

Apple Nut Salad

2-1/2 cups apples, diced
1/2 cup celery, finely chopped
1/4 cup walnuts, chopped
1/2 cup pecans, chopped
1/4 cup raisins
2/3 cup mayonnaise
1 tablespoon lemon juice
1/8 teaspoon salt
lettuce leaves

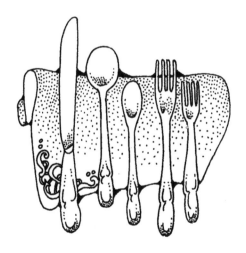

In a bowl, combine all the ingredients. Toss to mix well and then cover. Serve on crisp lettuce leaves. Serves 6.

Golden Red Fruit Salad

4 medium Golden Delicious apples, diced
4 medium Red Delicious apples, diced
2 cups seedless green grapes, halved
2 cups seedless red grapes, halved
1 can (20 ounces) pineapple chunks, drained
1 can (11 ounces) mandarin oranges, drained

Dressing:
1 package (3 ounces) cream cheese, softened
1/2 cup sour cream
1/2 cup mayonnaise
1/2 cup sugar

Combine all the fruit in a large bowl and chill. Meanwhile in a small mixing bowl, combine and beat all of the dressing ingredients until smooth. Pour this mixture over the fruit and toss gently until well-coated and serve. Makes 15-20 servings.

Apple Cheese Jello Salad

1 3-ounce package lemon-lime flavored gelatin
2 cups boiling water
1 cup apples, finely diced
3 ounces cream cheese
1/2 cup American cheese, shredded
1 cup seedless grapes, halved
1/4 cup pecans, chopped
lettuce leaves

Dissolve gelatin in boiling water. Chill 2/3 cup gelatin mixture until syrupy. Combine with diced apple. Pour into a 1-1/2 quart mold. Chill until set but not firm. To remaining gelatin mixture add the cream cheese, American Cheese, grapes and pecans. Beat until well blended. Carefully pour onto the apple gelatin mold. Chill until set. Unmold onto lettuce leaves. Serves 6.

Apple Broccoli Salad

6 medium tart apples, chopped
3 cups broccoli florets
1 small onion, chopped
1/2 cup raisins
1-1/2 cups mayonnaise
2 tablespoons white vinegar
1-1/2 teaspoons sugar
1/2 teaspoon lemon juice
1/2 teaspoon salt
10 bacon strips cooked and crumbled
1/2 cup walnuts, coarsely chopped

In a large bowl, combine the apples, broccoli, onion and raisins. In a small bowl, combine the mayonnaise, vinegar, sugar, lemon juice and salt. Pour this over the apple mixture and toss to coat. Cover and chill for at least 2 hours. Just before serving, stir in the bacon and walnuts. Makes 10-12 servings.

SIDE DISHES

Opportunities are seldom labeled.

Apple Wild Rice Pilaf

1/2 cup onion, chopped
1/2 cup celery, chopped
2 tablespoons butter or margarine
1-1/4 cups hot water
3/4 cup uncooked wild rice
1-1/2 teaspoons chicken bouillon granules
1 small red apple, chopped
2 tablespoons pecans, toasted and chopped
1/4 teaspoon grated lemon peel, optional

In a large saucepan over medium heat, sauté onion and celery in butter until tender. Stir in the water, rice and bouillon. Bring this mixture to a boil. Reduce heat, cover and simmer for 50 minutes or until the liquid is absorbed and the rice is tender. Remove from the heat and fold in the apple, pecans and lemon peel. Makes 4 servings.

Sauerkraut and Apples

1 bag of sauerkraut rinsed
1/2 a stick (4 tablespoons) of margarine
1/4 cup of water
3 apples, cored and quartered
1 or 2 large onions, cut into chunks
3 to 5 potatoes, peeled and cubed

Toss all of these ingredients into a crock pot on high for the day. Stir once in a while if you choose. Crock pots vary in size and heat. If needed turn your pot to low if cooking too fast. Cook to how you like your kraut done. This can also be done in an oven at 350° for 2 to 3-1/2 hours covered with foil.

Sausage Apple Stuffing

1/2 cup sausage
1/2 cup tart apples, chopped
1 tablespoon onion, chopped
1/4 teaspoon salt
1/8 teaspoon pepper
1/2 cup hot water
1/2 cup bread crumbs
1/2 cup cracker crumbs

In a frying pan, fry the sausage over medium heat until slightly brown. Do not drain. Add the remaining ingredients and mix well. This will stuff a game hen or pheasant. To do a 5 pound chicken, double this recipe.

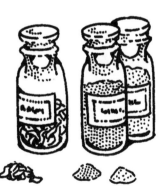

Apple Cider Sweet Potatoes

6 sweet potatoes, unpeeled and boiled
2/3 cup maple syrup
1 teaspoon salt
2 tablespoons butter
1 cup apple cider
1/3 cup water

Preheat oven to 300°. In a greased baking dish, cut the sweet potatoes into 1 inch slices. In a pot combine maple syrup, salt, butter, cider and water. Over medium heat bring this mixture to a boil, stirring occasionally. Pour this mixture over the potatoes and place them in the oven. Bake for 1 hour.

Hot Red Cabbage

2 tablespoons salad oil
1 medium head of red cabbage, shredded (about 4 cups)
2 medium apples, cored and chopped
2/3 cup vinegar
2 cups hot water
1/2 teaspoon salt
3 tablespoons sugar

Heat the oil in a pan, add all the ingredients and cook, stirring occasionally, until the apples are tender. Takes 20-30 minutes depending on the size of the pan. Serves 6 people.

Baked Apples With Onions

12 tart apples, peeled and sliced
3 onions, sliced
2 tablespoons butter
1 teaspoon salt
1/4 teaspoon pepper
1/2 cup dry breadcrumbs
1 tablespoon melted butter
1/2 cup water

Preheat the oven to 350°. In a greased baking dish, take 6 of the sliced apples and spread them out over the bottom of the pan. Top the apples with 1/2 of the onion slices, separated into rings. Dot with 1 tablespoon of butter. Sprinkle with 1/2 teaspoon salt and 1/8 teaspoon of pepper. Add the remaining apples, onions, butter and salt and pepper. In a cup combine the breadcrumbs and melted butter. Sprinkle this over the top, add water and cover. Bake for 2 hours or until tender. Serves 6.

Apple Raisin Stuffing

1 cup celery, chopped
1 cup onion, chopped
2 tablespoons butter or margarine
3 cups apples, peeled and chopped
2 cups raisins
8 cups day-old white bread, cubed
1 teaspoon salt
2-3 tablespoons sugar
2 eggs
1/2 cup apple cider
1/2 cup water

In a skillet over medium heat, melt the butter and sauté the celery and onion. When cooked, transfer this to a large bowl. Add the apples, raisins, bread, salt and sugar. In a small bowl, beat the eggs, cider and water. Pour this over the bread mixture and toss lightly. You can bake at 350° in bread pans for about 30-45 minutes, until golden brown. Also use as stuffing for your poultry or chops.

Fried Onions and Apples

4 large onions, sliced
3 tablespoons butter
6 large tart, red apples, cored and sliced
1/2 cup packed brown sugar
salt to taste

In a large sauté pan over medium heat, sauté the onions in the butter until just tender. Place the apples on top of the onions. Sprinkle the brown sugar and the salt over the apples. Cover and simmer for 10 minutes. Uncover and simmer 5 more minutes, until the apples are tender. This is a good compliment to pork.

Grandma's Red Cabbage

3 cups red cabbage, shredded
2 medium apples, cored and cubed
1/4 cup cider vinegar
1/4 cup brown sugar
1/4 cup water
1 teaspoon salt
1/8 teaspoon pepper
2 tablespoons bacon drippings or oil
dash of caraway seeds (optional)

In a large pot, over medium heat, combine all the ingredients and cover to steam. Cook 30-45 minutes, stirring occasionally, until tender. Serves 4.

Carrot Apple Whip

2 medium apples, pared and cored
8 medium carrots, peeled and sliced
3 tablespoons butter
salt and pepper to taste

Quarter the apples and place them in a small pot. Cook in a small amount of water until tender. When done, press the apples through a sieve, you need 1 cup. In another pot cook sliced carrots in salted water until tender and drain and mash, should measure 2 cups. Mix the apples and carrots. Add the butter and seasonings and whip until very light. Serves 6.

Apple Stuffing

1 cup butter, melted
6 cups tart apples, diced
1-1/2 cups onion, chopped
1-1/2 cups celery, chopped
2 teaspoons salt
1 cup sugar
6 cups small bread cubes

In a large frying pan, combine butter, apples, celery and onions. Sprinkle with salt and sugar. Cook for 10 minutes until apples are browned completely. Remove to a large bowl and add the bread cubes, tossing well. Makes 12 cups.

Scalloped Sweet Potatoes

1 18-ounce can of sweet potatoes, drained
1/4 cup orange juice
2-1/2 cups applesauce
1 teaspoon grated orange rind
1 teaspoon lemon juice
1 cup buttered breadcrumbs

Preheat oven to 350°. Place sweet potatoes in a greased casserole dish. In a bowl, combine remaining ingredients except the breadcrumbs. Pour the fruit mixture over the sweet potatoes and sprinkle the top with the breadcrumbs. Bake for 45 minutes to 1 hour or until hot and bubbly. Serves 6.

MAIN DISHES

An apology is a good way to have the last word.

Apple-Sausage-Sweet Potato Casserole

1 pound bulk pork sausage
1/4 cup water
1 can (23 ounces) sweet potatoes, drained and sliced thick
1/2 cup brown sugar
1/4 cup butter
3 medium cooking apples

Preheat oven to 350°. Form the sausage into 4 patties and brown in a skillet over medium heat and drain. Place the patties in the bottom of a 2-quart casserole dish and add the water. Layer slices of the sweet potatoes over the sausage and sprinkle with the sugar and 1/2 of the butter. Top with sliced unpeeled, cored apple rings, cut 1/2 inch thick. Dot with the remaining butter. Cover and bake for 30 minutes, then uncover and bake 15 minutes longer. Serves 4.

Pork Chops, Sausage and Apples

6 medium potatoes, peeled and cubed
6 apples, peeled, cored and cubed
2 medium onions, chopped
2 cups beef stock
1 teaspoon ground cinnamon
dash of salt and pepper
6 pork chops
12 fresh pork sausage links
2 tablespoons fresh parsley, chopped

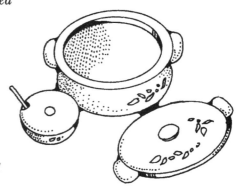

In a large pan combine the potatoes, apples, onions, beef stock, cinnamon, salt and pepper. Bring this mixture to a boil. Lower the heat and cook slowly for 40 minutes or until the potatoes are tender and most of the liquid is absorbed. Keep warm. In a frying pan, melt a small pat of butter or cooking fat, season the chops with salt and pepper and brown. Add 1/4 cup water; simmer covered for 30 minutes or until well done. Cook the pork sausage until well done and drain off the fat. On a warm platter arrange the meat and potato mixture. Sprinkle with parsley. Serves 6.

Apple Stuffed Game Hens

6 Cornish game hens
1 medium tart apple, sliced
1 medium white onion, sliced
1/4 cup butter or margarine, melted
1/4 cup soy sauce

Preheat oven to 350°. Wash and rinse your game hens and pat them dry. Mix the onion and apple together and divide it up into six mounds then loosely stuff each game hen. Combine the melted butter and soy sauce. Brush this over the hens. Bake uncovered for 50-60 minutes basting occasionally until done.

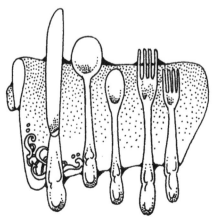

Squash and Sausage Balls

2 medium acorn squash
1 pound bulk pork sausage
2 cups sweetened applesauce
cinnamon to taste
salt

Preheat oven to 350°. Cut the squash lengthwise and remove the seeds. In a shallow baking dish place the squash cut side down and bake until almost tender, about 30-40 minutes. Meanwhile, form the sausage into small balls. Brown them over medium to low heat for about 15 minutes and drain. Add the applesauce and cinnamon to the pan and stir. Then add the sausage balls. Cover and simmer for 15 minutes. Remove your squash from the oven and turn them cut side up and sprinkle them with salt. Fill the cavity of the squash with the applesauce and sausage. Place back into the oven and continue baking until the squash is tender, about 20 minutes.

Apple Chops

8 pork chops
1/2 teaspoon salt
1/2 teaspoon sage
4 tart apples, cored and sliced
1/4 cup brown sugar
2 tablespoons flour
1 cup hot water
1 tablespoon vinegar
1/2 cup raisins, dried cherries, or dried cranberries

Preheat the oven to 350°. Spray a skillet with a non-stick spray. Season the pork chops with the salt and sage and brown in the skillet. When brown, place the chops in a baking dish, top with apples and sprinkle with the brown sugar. Going back to the frying pan, over medium heat, add the flour and blend well with the pan drippings to form a paste. Whisk in the water and vinegar until well blended and cook until it thickens. Add the dried fruit if desired and pour this mixture over the pork chops. Bake uncovered for 1 hour.

Turkey Apple Pie

9-inch pastry crust for a single pie crust
1/4 to 1/2 cup onion, chopped
1 tablespoon butter or margarine
1 can condensed cream of chicken soup
1 can condensed cream of mushroom soup
3 cups turkey or chicken, cooked and cubed
1 large tart apple, cubed
1 can of mushrooms
1 teaspoon pepper
1 teaspoon lemon juice

In a saucepan, over medium heat, sauté the onion in the butter until transparent. Add the soups, poultry, apple, mushrooms, pepper and lemon juice. Mix well. Preheat the oven to 400°. Pour the meat mixture into an 11 x 7 x 2 inch baking dish. Place the pastry to fit the top of the baking dish, cutting vents on the top. Bake for 30 minutes or until the crust is golden brown and the filling is bubbling. Serves 6.

Applesauce Glazed Ham

1/4 cup applesauce
1/3 cup honey
2 tablespoons prepared mustard
1 large ham steak, sliced 1/2 inch thick

Preheat the oven to 325°. In a bowl, combine the applesauce, honey and mustard. Place the ham steak in a baking dish and spread with the applesauce mixture. Place in the oven for 1 hour, basting occasionally.

Roast Duck

1 duck
salt
2-3 onions, quartered
2-3 apples, quartered
5 tablespoons butter, divided and melted
6 tablespoons currant jelly
1/4 teaspoon dry mustard
1/4 teaspoon salt
1 cup orange juice
1/2 teaspoon grated orange peel

Preheat the oven to 350°. Take the duck and rub the inside with salt. Combine the onion and apple and loosely stuff the duck, do not pack it tightly. In a baking dish (with a rack preferably) place the duck breast side down and baste with 2 tablespoons of the melted butter. Place in the oven to roast. In a bowl combine the remaining melted butter and the other ingredients over low heat, stirring until well blended. Keeping this mixture warm, baste the duck every 15 to 20 minutes. Roast the duck 45 minutes per pound.

Apple Stuffed Pork Sausage

1-1/2 pounds bulk pork sausage
1-1/2 cups apple, pared, cored and chopped
1/2 cup celery, chopped
1/4 cup onion, chopped
2 teaspoons minced parsley
1 cup dry breadcrumbs
3/4 teaspoon salt
1/4 teaspoon dry mustard
pepper to taste

Preheat the oven to 375°. Divide the sausage in half. Press half of the meat into a 9 inch pie pan. Take the meat from the pie pan and place it on the wax paper. Form another 9 inch round in the pan with the other half of the sausage meat, forming it to the sides and bottom of the pan. In a bowl combine the remaining ingredients to make the stuffing. Place this on the meat in the pie pan and top with the remaining sausage round. Press the meat together to seal. Place in an oven and bake for one hour. Remove from the oven and drain the fat. Slice and serve.

Fried Sausage and Apples

3 pounds sausage
4 apples, cored and cut into rings
brown sugar (enough to cover apples)
1 to 2 teaspoons cinnamon

Shape your sausage into patties. Over medium heat, in a large skillet, cook the patties until well done. Place the meat on a warm platter to keep warm. Keep about 1/2 inch of the pork fat in the pan and add the apple rings, sugar and cinnamon and cook, turning frequently until tender. Remove the pan from the heat and cover. Let set for 3 minutes. Uncover and return the apples back to the heat and cook until the apples are glazed. Add the apples to the warm patties and serve. 6 servings.

BREADS, MUFFINS
AND PANCAKES

*He who can take advice is sometimes
superior to him who can give it.*

Apple Bread

1/2 cup shortening
1 cup sugar
1-1/2 tablespoons buttermilk
2 eggs
1 teaspoon vanilla
1 teaspoon baking soda
1 teaspoon salt
1 cup apple cider
2 cups flour
1-1/2 cups apple, chopped
1/2 cup walnuts, chopped
2 teaspoons sugar
1/2 teaspoon cinnamon

Preheat the oven to 350°. In a bowl cream the shortening and sugar. Add the buttermilk, eggs and vanilla, blending well. Alternate adding the dry ingredients and cider into the mixture. Stir the apples and walnuts into the batter. Pour the batter into a greased loaf pan. Mix the sugar and cinnamon together and sprinkle over the batter. Bake for 1 hour and 15 minutes or until toothpick test done. Makes one loaf.

Baked Apple Gingerbread

6 apples, peeled, cored and cut into eights
1/2 cup sugar
1/4 cup water
1 cup molasses
1 beaten egg
1/2 cup melted butter
1 tablespoon ginger
1 teaspoon baking soda
1 cup hot water
2 cups sifted flour

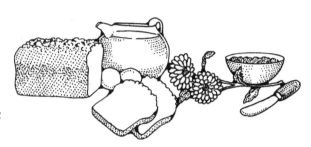

Preheat oven to 350°. Grease one loaf pan. In a medium saucepan combine the sugar, water and the apples. Cook for 3 minutes and drain. Place the apples in a greased loaf pan. In a bowl combine the remaining ingredients and beat this well. Pour this mixture over the apples. Bake for 40 minutes. Test with toothpick. Makes one loaf.

Apple Orange Bread

2 large tart apples, unpeeled, cored and quartered
1 large orange, unpeeled, quartered and seeded
1-1/2 cup raisins
2/3 cup shortening
2 cups sugar
4 eggs
1 teaspoon lemon extract
4 cups all-purpose flour
2 teaspoons baking powder
1-1/2 teaspoons baking soda
1 teaspoon salt
2/3 cup orange juice
1 cup walnuts, chopped

In a food processor or blender, place your apples, orange and raisins. Cover and process until finely chopped and set aside. In a large mixing bowl, cream the eggs, shortening, and sugar slowly, beating well. Beat this mixture until light and fluffy. Add the extract. Sift the dry ingredients in a separate bowl. Alternate the dry ingredients and the orange juice by adding them into the creamed mixture. Stir in the fruit and nuts. Pour the mixture into 3 greased loaf pans. Bake at 350° for 50 to 60 minutes. Done when toothpick inserted in the center comes out clean. Cool in pans for 10 minutes before removing to wire racks.

Canned Apple Nut Bread

4 cups sifted flour
1 cup sugar
6 teaspoons baking powder
2 teaspoons salt
1 teaspoon baking soda
1 can (1lb., 4 ounce) pie-sliced apples
1 cup milk
2 beaten eggs
1/2 cup melted butter
1 cup walnuts, chopped
2 tablespoons lemon juice

Preheat oven to 350°. In a large bowl combine the flour, sugar, baking powder, salt and baking soda. Drain the apples and set 10 slices aside for garnish. Dice the remaining apple slices. To the flour mixture add the apples, milk, eggs, melted butter, nuts and lemon juice. Mix until well blended. Grease two loaf pans and divide the batter mixture between the two pans. Bake for 50-60 minutes until brown and toothpick test comes clean. Remove from the oven and let stand for 10 minutes. Remove from pans to wire rack to cool Garnish with the apple slices.

Applesauce Loaf

1/2 cup shortening
1 cup sugar
2 eggs
1-3/4 cups sifted all-purpose flour
1 teaspoon salt
1 teaspoon baking powder
1/2 teaspoon baking soda
1/2 teaspoon cinnamon
1/2 teaspoon nutmeg
1 cup sweetened applesauce
1/2 cup walnuts, chopped

Preheat the oven to 350°. In a bowl with a mixer, beat the shortening and sugar until creamed. Add the eggs, beating until light and fluffy. Sift together the dry ingredients. Then add the dry ingredient and applesauce alternately to the creamed mixture until well mixed. Stir in the walnuts. Pour this mixture into a well greased loaf pan and bake for 1 hour. Remove from the oven and cool 10 minutes. Remove the bread from the pan and cool on a wire rack.

Cinnamon Sugar Applesauce Muffins

1/2 cup butter or margarine, softened
3/4 cup sugar, divided
2 eggs
3/4 cup applesauce
1-3/4 cups all-purpose flour
2 teaspoons baking soda
1/2 teaspoon salt
1/4 cup butter or margarine, melted
1/4 teaspoon ground cinnamon

Preheat the oven to 425°. In a bowl cream 1/2 cup butter, 1/2 cup sugar until light and fluffy. Add the eggs one at a time, beating well after each addition. Stir in applesauce. Combine the flour, baking soda and salt. Add this to the creamed butter and combine until moistened. Fill your greased muffin tins half full. Bake about 15 minutes or until done. Remove the muffins from the pans on cooling racks and set them upright. Combine the remaining 1/4 cup sugar and cinnamon. Brush the tops of the muffins with the melted butter and sprinkle with the cinnamon sugar.

Honey Apple Muffins

1 large apple, cored, pared and finely chopped
1-2/3 cups sifted flour
2 teaspoons baking powder
1 teaspoon cinnamon
1/4 teaspoon salt
1/4 cup sugar
1 tablespoon honey
1 beaten egg
2/3 cup milk
1/4 cup oil
6 tablespoons confectioners sugar

Preheat the oven to 375°. In a bowl, combine the flour, baking powder, cinnamon, salt and sugar. In another bowl, combine the honey, egg, milk and oil. Add the egg mixture to the flour mixture. Blend in the apple. Grease muffin tins and fill two-thirds full. For regular muffins bake for 20-25 minutes. Decrease the time for mini muffins and increase time for the jumbo muffins. Check with a toothpick, it is done when the toothpick comes out clean. Remove from the oven and let set for 5 minutes. Remove from the pans and sprinkle the tops with the confectioners sugar.

Apple Muffins

2 apples, pared, cored and finely chopped
2 cups sifted flour
2 teaspoons baking powder
1 teaspoon nutmeg
1/4 teaspoon cinnamon
1/2 teaspoon salt
2 tablespoons sugar
1 beaten egg
1 cup milk
1/4 cup oil

Preheat oven to 375°. In a medium bowl, add the flour, baking powder, nutmeg, cinnamon, salt and sugar and combine well. In a different bowl, combine the egg, milk and oil. Add the egg mixture to the flour mixture, and stir in the apples. Pour the batter into greased muffin tins. You can make any size muffins you choose, jumbo, regular or mini. Bake for approximately 35 minutes, add time for large muffins, subtract time for mini muffins. Use a toothpick to test, it is done when the toothpick comes out clean. Remove from the oven and let cool for 5 minutes. Remove from pans.

Apple Pancakes

1 cup sifted flour
1 teaspoon baking powder
1/2 teaspoon salt
2 teaspoons sugar
1 teaspoon cinnamon
1 beaten egg
1-1/2 cups milk
1 tablespoon oil
1/4 cup butter, melted
1 cup apple, pared, cored and chopped

In a bowl, combine the dry ingredients. In a separate bowl, combine the egg, milk, oil and butter. Add the wet mixture gradually to the dry ingredients. Stir until the batter is lumpy, then blend in the apples. With a large spoon drop the batter onto a hot, greased griddle. Cook until bubbles appear on the surface. Turn and cook until brown. These are good served with warm cinnamon applesauce.

Apple Sour Cream Pancakes

1-1/3 cups flour
1/2 teaspoon baking soda
1 teaspoon salt
1 tablespoon sugar
1/4 teaspoon nutmeg
1/4 teaspoon cinnamon or apple pie spice
1 beaten egg
1 cup sour cream
1 cup milk
1 cup apples, finely chopped
1/4 cup butter, melted

In a bowl, combine the dry ingredients thoroughly. In a different bowl, combine the egg, sour cream and milk. Blend this mixture into the flour mixture until lumpy. Mix the apples into the batter. On a hot greased griddle, spoon on or ladle the batter. Cook until bubbles appear on the surface of the pancakes. Turn them over and cook until brown. Serve with melted butter and syrup. Makes 10 to 12 pancakes.

PIES AND CRISPS

*A good rule for talking is one
used in measuring flour: sift first.*

Apple Cheese Pie

4 cups apples, pared, cored and sliced
3/4 to 1 cup sugar
2 tablespoons enriched flour
1/8 teaspoon salt
1 teaspoon cinnamon
1/4 teaspoon nutmeg
2 tablespoons butter

Cheese Pastry:
2 cups flour
1/2 teaspoon salt
1/2 cup grated sharp cheese
2/3 cup cold butter
4 to 5 tablespoons ice water

Preheat oven to 450°. In a bowl add the apples, sugar, flour, salt, cinnamon and nutmeg. Fill a 9 inch pie tin with the cheese pastry. Add the apples and dot with butter. Top the apples with the top pie pastry and seal. Cut some vents and bake for 10 minutes and then 40 minutes at 350°.

Cheese Pastry: Sift the flour and salt in a bowl. Stir in 1/2 cup grated cheese and cut in the butter until crumbly. Add the water and mix lightly with a fork, chill. Roll the pastry out.

Red Hot Apple Pie

1 pie crust recipe
6 medium apples, pared, cored and thinly sliced
3/4 cup sugar
1/2 cup water
1 4-ounce package red cinnamon candies
1 tablespoon flour
1 teaspoon lemon juice
1 tablespoon butter

Preheat oven to 450°. In a pan add the sugar, water and cinnamon candies. Cook over medium heat, stirring until the candies are dissolved. Add the apples and cook until the apples turn red. Drain and reserve the syrup. Blend the flour with 1/2 cup of the syrup and add the lemon juice. In an 8 inch pastry lined pie tin, add the apples, pour the syrup over the apples and dot with butter. Top with the pie crust and seal, making vent holes on the top crust for steam to escape. Bake in a 450° oven for 10 minutes and then 350° for 15 minutes.

Apple Pie

1 recipe for pie crust
5-7 tart apples, pared and sliced
3/4 to 1 cup sugar (depending on how tart you want the pie)
1 tablespoon lemon juice
2 tablespoons flour
1/8 teaspoon salt
1 teaspoon or more of cinnamon, depending on your taste
1/4 teaspoon nutmeg (optional)
2 tablespoons butter

Preheat oven to 450°. In a bowl, toss the apples, sugar, lemon juice, flour, salt and spices. Dump the apples into a 9 inch pastry lined pie pan. Dot the apples with butter and place the top crust over the apples and seal the crust by crimping or pinching it. Make a couple of slits on top of crust for venting. Bake at 450° for 10 minutes then at 350° for 40 minutes.

Scotch Apple Pie

5 apples for baking
3/4 cup brown sugar

Slice the apples and place them in a greased baking dish. Sprinkle the apples with brown sugar.

Topping:
3/4 cup packed brown sugar
1/2 cup butter or margarine
1 cup flour
pinch of salt
1/2 cup walnuts or pecans, chopped

Preheat the oven to 350°. In a bowl cream the butter and sugar until fluffy. Add the flour, salt and mix well. Stir in the nuts. Spread this mixture over the apples and sugar. Bake for 1 hour.

Carol's Apple Black Walnut Pie

1 pie crust (your favorite recipe)
apples, peeled, cored and sliced
1/2 cup sugar
1 teaspoon cinnamon

Crumb crust:
1/2 cup sugar
3/4 cup flour
1/2 to 1 cup black walnuts, chopped
1/3 cup butter

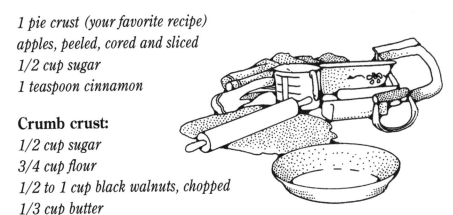

Place unbaked pie crust in a tin. Fill the pie crust with the apples and sprinkle them with the sugar and cinnamon mixed.

To make the crumb crust, combine the sugar, flour and walnuts, mix well. Cut in the butter and sprinkle over the apples. Bake at 450° for 10 minutes and then 350° for 35 minutes.

Recipe donated by Carol Geyer who runs the gift shop called "Memories" at the Lodge Bed and Breakfast in Presque Isle (Grand Lake) Michigan.

Apple Crumb Pie

4 large tart apples, pared, cored and sliced
1/2 recipe for pie crust or 1 prepared crust
1/2 cup sugar
1 teaspoon cinnamon
1/2 cup sugar
3/4 cup flour
1/3 cup butter
1 cup walnuts, chopped

Preheat the oven to 450°. Place the apples in a pie crust lined pie pan. Mix 1/2 cup of sugar with the cinnamon and sprinkle this over the apples. In a bowl, sift the remaining sugar and flour together. Cut the butter until crumbly and mix in the nuts. Take this mixture and sprinkle it over the apples. Bake at 450° for 10 minutes then 350° for 40 minutes or until the apples are tender.

Cherry Apple Crisp

3-4 medium apples, pared and cored
1 large can cherry pie filling or 2 cups pitted sweet cherries
1 cup rolled oats
1 cup brown sugar
3/4 cup flour
3/4 cup stick margarine or butter
1/2 to 1 cup walnuts, chopped

Preheat the oven to 350°. In a greased 9 x 13 inch baking pan, add your apples and cherries. In a bowl combine the oatmeal, sugar and flour. Cut in the butter to a cornmeal consistency and toss in the walnuts. Sprinkle this over the fruit and bake for 35 to 40 minutes.

Apple Crisp

3-4 medium apples, pared and cored
3/4 cup rolled oats
3/4 cup brown sugar
1/2 cup flour
1 to 2 teaspoons cinnamon
1/2 cup stick butter or margarine

Preheat the oven to 350°. In a greased baking pan (8 inch round), arrange your apple slices. In a bowl, combine the oatmeal, sugar, flour and spice. Cut in the butter and sprinkle over the apples. Bake for 35 to 40 minutes.

CAKES AND COOKIES

*Become the most positive and enthusiastic
person you know.*

Apple Streusel Coffee Cake

2-1/4 cups flour
3/4 cup sugar
3/4 cup butter
1/2 teaspoon baking powder
1/2 teaspoon soda
1 egg, beaten
3/4 cup buttermilk
1 can (20 ounces) apple pie filling
1/2 teaspoon grated lemon rind
1/2 teaspoon cinnamon
13 cup raisins (optional)

Preheat oven to 350°. Combine the flour and sugar in a large bowl. Cut in the butter until the mixture is crumbly. Set aside 1/2 cup of the mixture. To remainder, add the baking powder and soda and set aside. Combine the egg and buttermilk and add to the dry ingredients, stirring just until moistened. Spread two-thirds of the batter over the bottom and part way up the sides of a greased spring form pan. Combine the pie filling, lemon, cinnamon and raisins. Spoon this onto the batter in the pan, then drop spoonfuls of the batter over the filling. Sprinkle with reserved crumb mixture and bake for 1 hour.

Sour Cream Apple Bundt Cake

1/2 cup walnuts, chopped
1 teaspoon cinnamon
1/2 cup sugar
1/2 cup butter
1 cup sugar
2 cups flour
1 cup sour cream
2 eggs
1 teaspoon baking powder
1 teaspoon baking soda
1 teaspoon vanilla
1-1/2 cups apples, peeled, cored and finely chopped

Caramel Glaze Sauce:

3/4 cup brown sugar
2 tablespoons butter
1/2 teaspoon cinnamon
1/3 cup HOT evaporated milk

Preheat oven to 350°. In a small bowl, combine the nuts, cinnamon and sugar. Set aside. In a large bowl, cream the butter and sugar until light and fluffy. Add the flour, sour cream, eggs, baking powder, soda and vanilla and beat for 3 minutes. Grease and lightly flour a bundt pan. Spread 1/2 of the batter in the pan and then sprinkle the batter with 1/2 of the nut mixture and apples. Spread the rest of the batter into the pan and then the rest of the nut mixture. Bake for 60 minutes or until the cake begins to pull away from the sides of the pan. Make the caramel glaze by putting all the ingredients in a blender; covering and processing on high until the sugar is dissolved, set aside. Cool the cake some and remove it from the pan to a rack. Drizzle the glaze over the cake.

Apple Butter Cake

1 cup sugar	**Topping:**
1 stick butter	*5 tablespoons sugar*
2 eggs	*1 tablespoon cinnamon*
1 cup sour cream or sour milk	*1/2 to 1 cup chopped nuts*
2 cups flour	
1/2 teaspoon salt	
1 teaspoon baking soda	
3/4 cup apple butter	
1/2 to 1 cup chopped nuts	
1/2 teaspoon cinnamon	

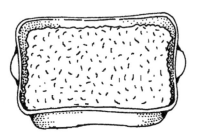

Preheat the oven to 350°. In a bowl, cream together the sugar and butter. Beat in the eggs and then the sour cream or sour milk. In a separate bowl, mix together the flour and salt, then add it to the sugar mixture until well blended. Stir in the baking soda, apple butter, nuts and cinnamon into the batter. Pour the batter into a greased 9 x 13 x 2 inch pan.

Topping: Mix the topping ingredients together in a bowl and sprinkle over the batter. Bake for 40 to 45 minutes.

Recipe donated by my friend Judy Adrian.

Applesauce Fruit Cake

3 cups sweetened applesauce
1 cup shortening
1/2 cup sugar
4-1/2 cups flour
4 teaspoons baking soda
1 teaspoon nutmeg
1/4 teaspoon cinnamon
1 pound mixed candied fruit
1 pound raisins
1/4 pound nuts

Preheat oven to 350°. In a saucepan, heat the applesauce, shortening and sugar, stirring until the sugar dissolves. Cool this mixture. In a bowl, sift the flour, soda, nutmeg and cinnamon. Stir in the applesauce mixture until well incorporated. Stir in the candied fruit, raisins and nuts. Grease two loaf pans, divide the batter into the pans and bake for 2 to 2-1/2 hours or until cake tests done.

Honey Applesauce Cake

2 eggs
1/2 cup shortening
1 cup honey
3 cups sifted flour
1-1/2 teaspoons baking soda
1/2 teaspoon salt
1 teaspoon cinnamon
1 teaspoon nutmeg
1/4 teaspoon cloves
1-1/2 cups applesauce
1/2 cup raisins
1/2 to 1 cup walnuts, chopped
powdered sugar

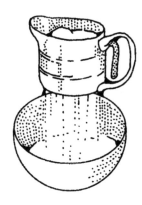

Preheat the oven to 350°. In a bowl, cream together the eggs, shortening and honey. Sift together the flour, soda and spices. Beat this into the creamed mixture alternately with the applesauce. Stir in the raisins and nuts. Pour the batter into a 9 x 13 x 2 inch pan and bake for 40 minutes. Cool and cut into squares. Dust with powdered sugar.

Apple Cookie Cake

1/4 cup shortening
1/2 cup sugar
1 egg
1/2 teaspoon vanilla
1-1/2 cups enriched flour
1/8 teaspoon salt
1-1/2 teaspoons baking powder
1/4 cup milk
4-5 apples, cored and sliced
1 cup sugar
1 tablespoon cinnamon
1 tablespoon flour

Preheat the oven to 400°. In a bowl, thoroughly cream the shortening and sugar. Add the egg and vanilla, beat well. In a bowl, sift the flour, salt and powder. Add the flour and milk alternately to the shortening, mixing well into a dough. Divide the dough in half and roll each piece into an 8 inch square. Line an 8 inch baking dish with one square. Arrange the apple slices over the dough. Mix the remaining ingredients and sprinkle over the apples, reserve 1/8 cup. Top with the remaining dough and sprinkle with the remaining sugar mixture. Bake for 40 minutes.

Apple-Nut Torte

4 eggs, well beaten
1-1/2 cups sugar
2/3 cup enriched flour
1 teaspoon baking powder
1/2 teaspoon salt
2 cups apple, peeled and chopped
1 cup walnuts, chopped

Preheat oven to 350°. With an electric mixer beat the eggs, then add the sugar. Beat on high speed for about 5 minutes until thick and light. In a separate bowl, sift together the flour, baking powder and salt. Add the dry ingredients into the egg mixture, then fold in the apples and nuts. Grease a 9 x 13 x 2 inch pan, pour the batter in and bake for 40 to 45 minutes. Cool and serve. Makes 8-10 servings.

Julie's Apple Cake

1-1/2 sticks of butter, softened
3/4 cup sugar
3 eggs, lightly beaten
1 teaspoon vanilla
1/2 teaspoon rum extract (optional)
1-1/2 cups white flour
3/4 teaspoon nutmeg
1/2 teaspoon baking powder
3 Golden Delicious apples
2 tablespoons lemon juice
2 tablespoons butter, melted
2 tablespoons sugar

Preheat oven to 400°. Spray or butter a 10 inch springform pan. With an electric mixer in a large bowl, cream together the 1-1/2 sticks of butter and the 3/4 cup sugar. Add the eggs, vanilla and rum flavoring and beat until light and fluffy. In a medium bowl, mix the flour, nutmeg and baking powder. Stir this mixture into the butter mixture (the batter will be stiff). Spread evenly into the springform pan.

Julie's Apple Cake, Continued

Peel the apples and place in a large bowl half-full with water and lemon juice. This will keep the apples from turning brown before you place them on the cake. Take each apple, one at a time, and cut in half lengthwise. Core each half, lay each half cut side down on a cutting surface and with a sharp knife slice each half crosswise into 1/4 inch slices. Keep the slices together in the apple shape. Lightly press each entire sliced half, cut side down, about halfway into the batter in the pan, spacing them evenly in a circle about 1 inch from the edge of the pan. Brush the exposed apple halves with the melted butter and sprinkle the entire top of the cake with sugar. Bake 30-35 minutes or until golden and apples are tender. Cool before cutting. Serve alone or with whipping cream.

Recipe donated by my friend Julie Robarge.

Apple Pound Cake

2 cups sugar
1-1/2 cups vegetable oil
3 eggs
2 teaspoons vanilla extract
3 cups all-purpose flour
1 teaspoon baking soda
1 teaspoon salt
1/2 teaspoon ground cinnamon
1/2 teaspoon nutmeg
2 cups tart apples, peeled and chopped
1 cup almonds, chopped
1/2 cup raisins

Apple Cider Glaze:
1/2 cup apple cider or juice
1/2 cup packed brown sugar
2 tablespoons butter or margarine

In a mixing bowl, combine sugar, oil, eggs and vanilla. Mix well. Combine the flour, baking soda, salt, cinnamon and nutmeg. Add this to the egg mixture and mix well. Stir in the apples, almonds and raisins. Pour into a greased and floured 10 inch fluted tube pan. Bake at 350° for 1-1/4 to 1-1/2 hours or until a toothpick comes out clean. Cool for 15 minutes before removing from the pan to a wire rack to cool completely.

In a saucepan, combine glaze ingredients. Cook over low heat until sugar is dissolved. Prick top of cake with a fork and drizzle with the glaze. Makes 16 servings.

Apple Cake

2 cups sugar
1-1/2 cups vegetable oil
2 eggs
3 cups flour
1/2 teaspoon baking soda
1/2 teaspoon salt
2 teaspoons cinnamon
3 cups apples, cored and coarsely chopped
1 cup nuts, chopped
3/4 cup raisins

Preheat the oven to 350°. In a bowl, blend the sugar, oil and eggs. In a separate bowl, mix together the flour, soda, salt and cinnamon. Then add this mixture to the sugar mixture. By hand add the apples, nuts and raisins. The batter will be very thick. In a very well greased tube cake pan, add the batter and press it down into the pan. Bake about 1-1/2 hours. Cool before taking it out of the pan.

This recipe is donated by my friend and son's God Mother Karen Frampton.

Iced Apple Cookies

2 cups all-purpose flour
1 teaspoon baking soda
1 teaspoon cinnamon
1/2 teaspoon salt
1/4 teaspoon cloves
1/4 teaspoon nutmeg
1-1/3 cups light brown sugar, packed
3/4 cup plus 2 tablespoons unsalted butter, softened
1 large egg
1 cup pecans
1 cup raisins
1 cup delicious apple, chopped
1/2 cup plus 2 tablespoons apple cider
3 cups confectioners sugar

Preheat the oven to 350°. Mix first 6 dry ingredients together. Cream the sugar and 3/4 cup butter until fluffy. Add the egg, mixing well. Gradually add the flour mixture until well combine. Stir in the pecans, raisins, apples and 1/4 cup of the apple cider until well combined. On an ungreased cookie sheet, drop the dough by tablespoons and flatten slightly. Bake for 18 to 20 minutes. Cool on a wire rack. In a small bowl stir together the confectioners sugar, remaining cider and butter until smooth. Drizzle about 1 tablespoon of the icing over each cookie. Store in an airtight container for up to 4 days. Makes 12-15 cookies.

Applesauce Drops

1/2 cup butter, softened
1 cup sugar
1 egg
1 cup sifted flour
1 tablespoon baking powder
1/2 teaspoon salt
1 teaspoon cinnamon
1/2 teaspoon cloves
1 teaspoon nutmeg
1 cup applesauce
1 cup raisins
1-3/4 cups rolled oats

Preheat oven to 375°. In a bowl, combine the butter and sugar until creamed. Beat in the egg. In a separate bowl combine all the dry ingredients except the rolled oats. Stir this mixture into the butter mixture and mix thoroughly. Mix in the applesauce and add the rolled oats last. Using a teaspoon, drop the cookie batter onto a greased cookie sheet. Bake for 15 minutes or until brown. Makes 5 dozen.

DESSERTS

Be patient with the faults of others,
they have to be patient with yours.

Old Fashioned Carmel Apples

6 medium red apples
1 cup sugar
3/4 cup dark corn syrup
1 cup light cream
2 tablespoons butter
1 teaspoon vanilla extract
wooden skewers or popsicle sticks
candy thermometer
crushed nuts or candy pieces (optional)

Stick wooden skewers into the stem end of the apples. In a heavy pot combine the sugar, corn syrup, cream and butter. Cook over low heat until the sugar dissolves. Cook to very hardball stage (254-260°) without stirring. Remove from heat, add vanilla and dip the apples into syrup. You will have to dip fast. If you desire, roll the apple in chopped nuts or candy pieces. Place upright on well-greased cookie sheet to cool. You can also dip the apples in different chocolates.

Apple Dumpling

2 cups sugar
2 cups water
1/4 teaspoon cinnamon
1/4 teaspoon nutmeg
1/4 cup butter
2 cups flour
1 teaspoon salt
2 teaspoons baking powder
3/4 cup shortening
1/2 cup milk
6 apples, pared, cored and cut into quarters
mixture of cinnamon, sugar and nutmeg

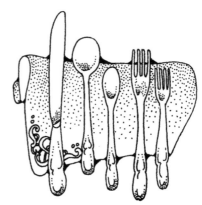

Preheat oven to 375°. In a saucepan over medium heat, make a syrup with the first 4 ingredients. Then stir in the butter to melt. Sift the flour, salt and baking powder, then cut in the shortening. Add the milk all at once to moisten to dough consistency. Roll the dough out on a floured area to make 6, 1/4 inch thick by 5 inch squares. Arrange 4 pieces of apple on each square and sprinkle generously with the sugar mixture. Dot with butter, fold the corners to the center and pinch the edges together. Place the dumplings one inch apart on a greased baking pan. Pour the syrup over the dumplings and bake for 35 minutes.

Crunch Applesauce Bars

1 cup sugar
1 cup unsweetened applesauce
1/2 cup shortening
2 cups enriched flour, sifted
1 teaspoon soda
1-1/2 teaspoons cinnamon
1 teaspoon nutmeg
dash of cloves
1/4 teaspoon salt
1 cup raisins
1/4 cup walnuts, chopped
1 teaspoon vanilla

Topping:
2/3 cup corn flakes, crushed
1/4 cup sugar
1/4 cup walnuts, chopped
2 tablespoons butter or
   margarine, softened

Preheat oven to 350°. In a bowl, combine the sugar and applesauce. Add the shortening and blend. In a separate bowl, sift together the flour, soda, spices and salt. Add this to the applesauce mixture and stir until smooth. Add the raisins, nuts and vanilla. Spread the batter into a greased 15-1/2 x 10-1/2 x 1 inch jelly roll pan. Combine the topping ingredients in a bowl and sprinkle this over the batter. Bake for 30 minutes or until done. Makes 32 bars.

Apple Bread Pudding

4 cups soft bread crumbs
1 cup apples, peeled, cored and diced
2 cups scalded milk
2 tablespoons butter, melted
3 eggs
1/2 cup sugar
1 teaspoon vanilla
1 teaspoon cinnamon
1/4 teaspoon nutmeg
1/4 teaspoon cloves
1 teaspoon lemon rind, grated

Preheat oven to 350°. In a bowl, mix the bread and the apples and set aside. Combine milk, butter, eggs, sugar, vanilla, cinnamon, nutmeg, clove, and rind. After mixing well, pour over the apple bread mixture. Then spoon this mixture into a buttered 2-quart casserole dish. Set the dish in a larger pan filled with hot water and bake for 1 hour or until a knife inserted into the center comes out clean. Serve warm, makes 6 servings.

Butterscotch Apple Squares

2 cups sugar
2 eggs
3/4 cup vegetable oil
2-1/2 cups flour
1 tablespoon baking powder
1 teaspoon salt
1 teaspoon cinnamon
3 cups tart apples, diced
1 cup walnuts, chopped
1 cup butterscotch chips

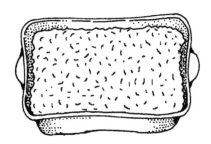

Preheat the oven to 350°. Grease a 13 x 9 x 2 inch baking pan. In a bowl, combine the sugar, eggs and oil, mixing well. Stir in the flour, baking powder, salt and cinnamon. This batter will be thick. Fold in the apples and nuts. Spread into the baking pan and sprinkle with the chips. Bake for 35 to 40 minutes or until golden and tooth pick comes out clean. Cool. Makes about 2 dozen.

Apple Soufflé

2 cups graham cracker crumbs (cinnamon graham crackers can be used)
1/2 teaspoon cinnamon
2 tablespoons butter, melted
3 egg yokes
1 15-ounce can sweetened condensed milk
2 tablespoons lemon juice
1 tablespoon lemon peel, grated
2 cups applesauce
3 egg whites, stiffly beaten

Preheat the oven to 350°. In a bowl, combine the graham cracker crumbs, cinnamon and butter. Spread the crumbs into an 8 inch baking dish, reserving a 1/4 cup of the crumbs. In a bowl, beat the egg yolks until a thick lemon color. Stir in the milk, lemon juice, lemon peel and applesauce. Gently fold the stiff beaten egg whites into this mixture and pour into the baking dish. Sprinkle the remaining crumbs over the mixture and bake for 50 minutes.

Old Fashioned Apple Candy

8 large tart apples, cored and sliced
1/2 cup water
2 cups sugar
2/3 cup red hot cinnamon candies
1 tablespoon or 1 envelope unflavored gelatin
1/4 cup cold water
granulated sugar

In a medium pot, place the apples and 1/2 cup water and cover. Cook until the apples are tender. Put the apples through a sieve to make 4 cups of applesauce. Add the sugar and cinnamon candies and return back to the pan and cook uncovered for 45 minutes over medium heat. In a small bowl, add the 1/4 cup water to the gelatin to soften. Add this to the hot mixture and cook for 20 minutes, stirring constantly. Pour into a greased 8 inch square pan and cool. When cool, cut in pieces and dip in granulated sugar. Store covered in a cool place. Let set for a day before eating. Makes about 18 pieces depending on the size you want the candy to be.

Apple Fritters

2 cups Bisquick® baking mix
1/2 cup sugar
2 large apples, peeled, cored and chopped
1 large egg
1/4 cup milk
cinnamon and sugar mixture

Heat an electric frying pan to 375°. Add 1-1/2 to 2 inches of oil. In a bowl, mix all the ingredients except the cinnamon sugar, to form a batter. Drop by spoonfuls into the hot oil, leaving space between to turn the fritter. Fry for 1-1/2 minutes on each side. Drain on paper towels and sprinkle with the cinnamon sugar.

Honey Baked Apples

6 medium baking apples
1-1/2 tablespoons butter, melted
1/4 cup honey
3/4 cup Grape Nut® cereal
1/4 cup raisins

Preheat the oven to 400°. Wash and core the apples. Peel the top half or slit the apple peel horizontally around each apple about 1 inch from the top to allow steam to escape. Place on a baking dish lined with tin foil. Bake for 40 minutes. Combine the butter, honey, cereal and raisins. Fill the apples with this mixture and bake for 10 more minutes. Serves 6.

Apple Oatmeal Bars

1 cup flour
1/2 teaspoon salt
1/2 teaspoon baking soda
1/2 cup brown sugar
1-1/2 cups rolled oats
1/2 cup butter
3 cups apples, peeled, cored and chopped
1/2 teaspoon cinnamon
1/2 cup sugar

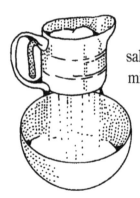

Preheat the oven to 350°. In a bowl, sift the flour, salt and soda. Add the brown sugar and rolled oats and mix well. Work the butter into this mixture. Grease a 9 x 13 inch baking pan and spread the mixture into the bottom of the pan. Spread the apples over the crust mixture, mix the cinnamon and sugar together and sprinkle over the apples. Bake for 40-45 minutes.

Stewed Apples

4 medium apples, cored and sliced
1/4 cup sugar
1/2 inch stick of cinnamon, optional

In a pot add the apples and a small amount of water, cover and cook slowly until tender. Add the sugar and cinnamon stick and continue cooking until the sugar dissolves. Serve warm.

Apple Pie Bars

Crust:
2 cups flour
1/2 cup sugar
1/2 teaspoon baking powder
1/2 teaspoon salt
1 cup butter
2 egg yokes, beaten

Crust: Combine flour, sugar, baking powder and salt. Mix well. Cut the butter into this mixture until crumbly. Mix the egg yolks in until combined. Press half of the mixture in the bottom of a 15 x 10 inch jelly roll pan or a 13 x 9 x 2 inch pan. Set the other 1/2 of the mixture aside.

Filling:
4 cups baking apples, pared, cored and thinly sliced
1/2 cup brown sugar
1/4 cup flour
1 teaspoon cinnamon
1/4 teaspoon nutmeg
2 egg whites, slightly beaten

Apple Pie Bars, Continued

Filling: Combine all the ingredients except the egg whites and arrange over the bottom crust. Crumble the remaining crust mixture over the filling. Brush the egg whites over the crumb crust. Bake at 350° for 30 to 40 minutes and cool. If desired, make confectioners sugar glaze and drizzle over the bars. Makes 3 to 4 dozen bars.

Glaze:
1/2 pound box confectioners powdered sugar
1 teaspoon vanilla
4 tablespoons milk, more if needed

In a bowl, mix the sugar and vanilla. Start adding the milk until it is a consistency that can be drizzled over the bars.

Red Hot Apples

6 medium tart apples
1/2 cup sugar
1/4 cup red hot candies
1/4 teaspoon ground cinnamon

Preheat oven to 350°. Grease an 8 inch square baking pan. Start by cutting the tops off the apples and set them aside. Then core the apples to within 1/2 inch of the bottom of the inside of the apple and set in the baking pan. In a bowl, combine the sugar, candies and cinnamon, then spoon 2 tablespoons into each apple. Replace the tops. Spoon any remaining sugar mixture over the apples. Bake uncovered for 30 minutes or until the apples are tender, basting occasionally.

Apple Raspberry Streusel Bars

2-1/2 cups plus 2 tablespoons all-purpose flour, divided
2 cups old fashioned rolled oats
1-1/4 cups sugar
2 teaspoons baking powder
1 teaspoon ground cinnamon
1 cup butter or margarine, melted
3 cups tart apples, peeled and thinly sliced
1 12-ounce jar raspberry preserves
1/2 cup walnuts, finely chopped

Preheat the oven to 375°. Grease a 13 x 9 x 2 inch pan. In a bowl, combine 2-1/2 cups flour, oats, sugar, baking powder and cinnamon. Mix in the butter, just until moistened. Set aside 2 cups for topping. Pat the remaining oat mixture into the baking pan and bake for 15 minutes. While this is baking, place the apples in a bowl and toss them with the 2 tablespoons of flour. Stir in the preserves and spread this mixture over the hot crust to within a 1/2 inch of the edges. Combine the nuts with the reserved oat mixture and sprinkle over the fruit mixture. Bake for another 30-35 minutes, until light brown.

Trail Mix

1 cup dried apple
1 cup dried cherries
1 cup dried apricots
1 cup dried banana chips
1 cup dried cranberries
1 cup dates
1 cup raisins
1 cup flaked coconut
1 cup shelled sunflower seeds
1 cup soy nuts
1 cup shelled peanuts
1 cup small carob chips
1 cup almonds

In a large storage bag, add all of the ingredients and shake well to mix. Store in ziplock bag or airtight containers in cool area. If stored properly, this mix can last for up to 6 months.

Apple Pudding

6 large apples, pared, cored and sliced
2 tablespoons lemon juice
1/4 cup water
1/2 teaspoon cinnamon
1 cup sugar, divided
3/4 cup flour
1/4 teaspoon salt
6 tablespoons butter or margarine

Preheat the oven to 375°. In a greased casserole dish, place your apples. In a small bowl mix together the lemon juice, water, cinnamon and 1/2 cup sugar. Add this to the apples and toss gently to just work it in. Combine the remaining sugar with the flour and salt, work in the butter using a pastry blender or fork until it resembles coarse cornmeal. Sprinkle this over the apples and pat smooth. Bake for 40 minutes or until the apples are tender and the crust is crisp and golden brown. Serves 6.

Baked Apples

Large, good quality baking apples, wash them and remove the core. Place the apples in a deep baking pan. In the center of each apple, place 1 to 2 tablespoons of brown sugar or white sugar and 1/2 teaspoon butter. Pour 1 cup of water around the apples and bake covered at 375° for about 45 minutes or until tender. If you choose, you can also add the following to the center of the apples with the sugar: chopped dates, raisins, mincemeat, nuts, cranberries, dried figs or other dried fruits. Be creative and choose what your taste buds enjoy.

INDEX

From small beginnings come great things. Proverbs

101 Apple Recipes

Life's Little Apple Cookbook

Notes

Notes

Favorite Recipes

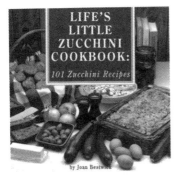

ISBN 0-932212-94-8

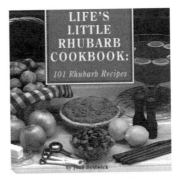

ISBN 1-892384-00-0

Look for Joan Bestwick's *Life's Little Zucchini Cookbook, Life's Little Rhubarb Cookbook, Life's Little Berry Cookbook* and *Life's Little Peaches, Pears, Plums & Prunes Cookbook* also by Avery Color Studios, Inc.

ISBN 1-892384-05-1

ISBN 1-892384-11-6

Avery Color Studios, Inc. has a full line of Great Lakes oriented books, puzzles, cookbooks, shipwreck and lighthouse maps, and lighthouse posters.

For a full color catalog call:
1-800-722-9925

Avery Color Studios, Inc. products are available at gift shops and bookstores throughout the Great Lakes region.